Drumming the Beat to Our Emotions

Poetry by
Two Inspiring
Garifuna Poets

By: Mirta Alicia Castillo
Co-author: Jose Valentin

AuthorHouse™ LLC
1663 Liberty Drive
Bloomington, IN 47403
www.authorhouse.com
Phone: 1-800-839-8640

Published by AuthorHouse 08/20/2014

ISBN: 978-1-4969-2447-6 (sc)
ISBN: 978-1-4969-2448-3 (e)

Library of Congress Control Number: 2014912089

This book is printed on acid-free paper.

ACKNOWLEDGEMENTS

Mirta Alicia Castillo:

I give special thanks first and foremost to my Creator, Jesus Christ, the one who is able to make the impossible, possible. I am and always will be eternally thankful to my deceased parents, for they taught me the true definition of literature enjoyment and the value of education, for they did not have the opportunity to do so themselves. *Drumming The Beat To Our Emotions* is a dedication of my love for them, and their memory. As I accomplished my career in nursing, it enabled me to live life to the fullest and also have enough love to be able to care for them as well, during their period of ailments. There was always a piece of me that never felt complete, but I knew my nursing career was fulfilling enough for the time being. I, however, used to enjoy writing but never acknowledged it enough for it to be part of my life. I am thankful to my siblings, Irma Castillo, Jorge Castillo, Samuel Castillo and Astrid Castillo for their on-going support and encouragement. To my sister Irma Castillo, I give special thanks because she always find time during the day to edge me on. I always look for her likes and comments on GTVP (GarifunaTv Page) for her daily cheers and words of encouragement! I am very thankful to God for being Garifuna. It was during the many years, decades, and centuries of oppression of the Garifuna people that also pushed me to write for my Garifuna culture. All of the discrimination we face, and inequalities were enough reasons to get me to express myself through writing. I discovered my abilities to write, as I communicated with a cousin of mine. My cousin and I had conversations and exchanges of e-mails that brought everything to light. Prior to this time, I just enjoyed writing, now I really love to write. I'm thankful to the founder of GarifunaTV Page Julian Rochez, also known as Don Juleon for he served as a mentor to me during the most difficult moments in my life, death of both parents and my divorce. I'm most thankful to Don Juleon, for all graphic work done online, and for *Drumming The Beat To Our Emotions*. GarifunaTV Page served as a sponge that absorbed the tears of my sorrows during those moments. I am thankful to everyone on GarifunaTV Page on Facebook, who support Poetry Nights and all of our poets week by week. Thanks to everyone who shared or sent a word of inspiration my way, for when it was done, it lifted my spirits edging me to continue and kept me inching forward. I am also thankful to my friend, Rose Avellanet for she believed in my abilities and always encouraged me to pursue writing, and shared moments with me when I truly needed it most, and giving me the most sympathetic words of encouragement to keep pressing forward. She was the one who encouraged me to get into competitions of my poetry, henceforth, my first poetry publication. Thank you Rose Avellanet for your friendship, and your encouragement. May God bless everyone who supported me through poetry on GarifunaTV Page and also through *Drumming The Beat To Our Emotions*.

Jose Valentin:

I would like to thank the Garifuna culture for helping me discover who I am. I would also like to thank GarifunaTV Page for having a forum for Garifuna like myself to express our thoughts and opinions that affect our community.

SPECIAL THANKS

First and foremost to my Heavenly Father, Jesus Christ and then to everyone who have supported GarifunaTv Page on Facebook, I say to you, thank you! GarifunaTv Page and Poetic Wednesdays was the stage that led to the production of "Drumming The Beat To Our Emotions". The Co-Author Jose Valentin and I in a million years would have never imagined it to have turned out this way. I, Mirta Alicia Castillo and Jose Valentin thank you all for your continued support. God is good, all the time!

In memory of my deceased parents, Silvio Castillo and Teofila Castillo, I dedicate "Drumming The Beat To Our Emotions" My father was always into literature and reading. I used to watch him do so all the time. Although he did not go to higher education, however, he pulled himself into that mode, and demonstrated to us, that we, his children can also accomplish it. He used to study the word of God, and graduated from the Bible Institute. His struggle remained with me. When he passed away, and the sorrows from my failing marriage, was what brought me into writing poetry. My mother was my biggest cheerleader, and always told me, "Daughter you can! Anything you put your mind to do, believe in God, and you shall." I loved my parents so much. This was the greatest pain I've ever endured in my entire lifetime. Thank God for them, and the love they had for one another, and my siblings.

To my niece Vanessa Castillo, and my sister, Irma Castillo I am grateful that God blessed me with you guys. Your immense support means the world to me. To Michael Morel, thank you for your support also, I love you guys to pieces. Thanks for believing in me.

To my niece Tania Flores, my Garifuna diva, the go-getter, the spunk of Miami, Florida and now Washington DC. You brighten and lift up moods, and spirits, and are fun to be around. Since you were a little girl. I am blessed to see you develop into a beautiful young woman, determined in what she believes and wants out of life. Thank you for your on-going support of "Drumming The Beat To Our Emotions".

To Virginia Johns and Tri-Shone Randall, thank you from the bottom of my heart. Virginia, you are one of the nicest persons I know, and your heart is gold! I love you girl! Thank you for your support, and follow through.

To Julian Rochez, AKA Don Juleon, thank you! Thank you for believing in me, your words of encouragement when I underwent the worst times in my life. You have showed me the true meaning of brotherhood. The amazing graphic work throughout "Drumming The Beat To Our Emotions" was created by Don Juleon. We have come a long way my brother, thank you!

To the entire poetry team on GarifunaTv Page, thank you! Also, to all of the Garifuna poets who partook in GarifunaTv thank you! Thanks for your continued devotion to Garifuna culture! We will continue working toward more publications by Garifuna!

To Jose Valentin, the Co-author of "Drumming The Beat To Our Emotions" thank you ever so much for believing in the poetry team. Despite the fact you are preparing yourself to become a lawyer, you still believed on Poetic Wednesdays, and never missed a day at submission. Thank you for being my right hand, and for being a true leader of the pack!

Contents

CELEBRATIONS

Flowery Occasions

Earth's most abundant essence,
Given at treacherous moments, aiding in the uplift of love's convalescence,

Women expect flowers at all times, but men's flowery occasions become lame,
Given to whirl women into the web of a new relationship, what a freaking shame!

All that is new, blossoming with fragrance and color, should be kept consistent,
Instead it is used as bandaid to patch-up deep wounds that remain persistent,

Track bouquets as they come, occasionally unsure of reasoning, how sad!
Sixth sense never lie, foolish of men to think it was overseen, must be mad!

Just as they thought it was missed, there goes another flowery occasion,
Awful to meet cheap men, won't share even for the sake of passion,

Machismo roles played determines who reels the next woman into the trap,
Meeting next macho man, you learn they feed-off the same literature of crap,

Women, much happier if the ideal of flowery occasions was more for true loving,
Where flowers represent a blossoming relationship, with lots of understanding,

Change ideals of flowery occasions, share it because it stems from the heart,
Let it not be for cover-up or stunting relational growth, or to outsmart,

Flowery occasions ought to come from deep within, to make us blossom farther in love!

Flowery Occasions

MIRTA ALICIA CASTILLO

Holiday Love

Family may irk a nerve here and there,

May even make you drop tears over the years,

Regardless what they do, family warmth is unique,

No better reward than that of family love,

After all the hurt, forgiveness is most rewarding,

Argue, curse, bad-mouthing do not equate making-up,

Sincere hugs, forgiveness and thankfulness renew us,

Travel across miles and oceans to gather,

All is worthwhile when you spend it together,

Lets love one other through the holiday season,

Allowing holiday seasons to repair broken bonds,

Holiday love is the best love we can ever experience!
Mirta Alicia Castillo

Holiday ♡ Love

MIRTA ALICIA CASTILLO

I Welcome You

Yesterday might have been partially blue,
But this one thing stands true,

There is not a thing that last an eternity,
Even as you arrived, you came purposely,

My heart sings as I see endless possibilities,
Brain will no longer work with disabilities,

I am able, is my affirmation for this time period,
For God lives in me, and it is almost always granted,

Won't deal like last year,
Lessons learned and will now be dealt with great cheer,

Come what may, or screw up however I may,
God has my best interest every day,

God, I thank you for another year,
I welcome you more for endless possibilities!

I
Welcome
You

Mirta Alicia Castillo

Merry Christmas My Love!

I've had Christmas' for many years
Some significant of mention, as this one nears

I truly dare you to make this one utterly different
Stamp this one with the seal of love, steamy, and yet ardent

Love that send electrifying chills through this aching body
Keeping me oooooh, ever anticipating and yet keeping me calmly

Brighten the dimness within the most intricate part of me
Adorn my heart with warmth like never before

Give me the merriest Christmas my love!

MERRY CHRISTMAS MY LOVE

Mirta Alicia Castillo

We Are The Only Ones Who Understand

It is here again, a month of jubilee, as the world cheer

We celebrate the world's radiant skin, and struggle
linked with it
Privileged after all inequities thrust at our forefathers

God knew it wasn't fair, his children yet suffered

He facilitated a way out, though there are still some
resisting
All there is left for them to do is hate

There is no more touching the children of the Most
High
Watch us walk, watch us do, watch us school, watch
us outdo

Blame us not for God's perfect creation

Despite the hatred, he loves us, despite the hurt, he
shields us
Despite being thrown out of our lands, he provided us shelter

He created master minds to surf the ocean body and
rescue his people to a much kinder land

He illuminated minds to use mother nature, using palm
trees, and twigs, mud, to make our humble homes

There is always reason to celebrate year in, and year
out, for our forefathers deserve the applause they
never received.

So we think we have it bad now, not as bad as our
forefathers!
Let's applaud the struggle, the victory and the
sustenance of our Blackness

We deserve to stand tall, proud, with great prestige,
most importantly with our taut Black and beautiful skin

Whoever don't like it, can step to the side, because
we are the outcome of our Black History!
After all, we are the only ones who understand!

We are the only ones who understand

MIRTA ALICIA CASTILLO

You Are Cordially Invited

It is known, rain and thunder only lasts a while,

As track of tears wash away, flaunting this new smile,

You are cordially invited in observance of the new me,

Observance of written eloquence, for I am free,

Free to express the negativity that once had hold, so that I and others learn,

You are cordially invited to hear expressions thereof,

Papi did you say dinner, and you are going to pay?

Handsome pulling out $100 bill, I may want you to stay,

You are cordially invited to see the joy,

Joy no one can steal, but joy that only God provide,

Joy that can only be shared with someone, in who you
can confide

This is the home only the joyous can reside,

You are cordially invited to see the brightness of future,

Where only God reigns, and we follow,

A man happy to have me as wife, without turning to look at another,
being that typical fellow,

Respect without using foulness, instead that of edification,

If ready to build in this future, you are cordially invited to partake in
this celebration,

Otherwise, doors have two ways in which it allows access,

Lets see how well we progress,

You are cordially invited!

MIRTA ALICIA CASTILLO

Most Memorable and Treasured Celebration

Gray skies brightened by sunny rays of light

Puddles where pouring rain didn't avail for this season

Just like streams of tears shed for one's most dear

A year gone by with occasional tears of remembrance

Remembrance of the greatest blessings endured

No more tears of loss instead that of celebration

Celebrating immense life given, loved, and shared
Fond memories and pictures of every rich moment

Biography of events, love, teachings, and guidance

Learning all beautiful things last forever just like God

Crucial memory, heart and the sense of belonging

Relying on memory not failing, is all I do to envision

Vivid picture and the play of the best video of my life

Outpour of joy that will always dwell within forever

God giveth and God taketh, law of life ready or not

Now I am ready as God also pulled me through the

Greatest pain ever, more reason for rejoicing!

Mirta Alicia Castillo

CULTURE

Garifuna Nation

Awesome is the day we finally accept totally, being Garifuna,
Not the country that once gave us refuge, but true to the ones that accepted our difference,

Breaking down the divisive walls of being Honduran, Belizian, Guatemalan, or Nicaraguan,

We are Garifuna, the ingredient we all have in common,
The Garifuna that longs to come together every time,

Separatism and language walls crumbling to unify fronts,
Realizing we are all equally Garifuna, educationally or not,

Supporting each other's efforts until majority excel,
Lifting one another so that the next generation mimic well,

Creating and supporting Garifuna-based businesses,
Initiate electoral process to generate specific Garifuna consciousness,

Include all Garifuna worldwide regardless of geographical location,
This is the Garifuna Nation that I envision, oh what pride it will be!

THE GARIFUNA NATION

MIRTA ALICIA CASTILLO

Garifuna Roots

Garifuna upbringing; born and raised a Harlem resident.
Born on the day of the veterans.
My mom made, my aunt named me; still society try to enslave me.
To that system we call the penitentiary.
My cell will continue to remain empty.
Too often provoked.
The consequence is returning broke and unable to vote.
Leaving a man with no hope.
The values instilled, deflects any stone my mind has build.
I have learned the importance of the word "able".
So much in life is actually attainable.
Critics are often inescapable.
Question I ask is, I'm changing for who?
I guess no one believed in them.
So attempts are made to drag me down this historical trend.
Economic disparity in wealth.
Affirmative Action unable to deter the resumes collecting dust on the shelf.
Is like a fight from all angles.
Another web is created after each one I untangle.
I have a strong belief in optimism.
Garifuna roots provided with me priceless wisdom.
I come from people who built houses and survived through the art of fishing.
Every dugu, I learn to be caring and giving.
I'm thankful for the values embedded in me.
Being Garifuna is the reason physically and mentally free.

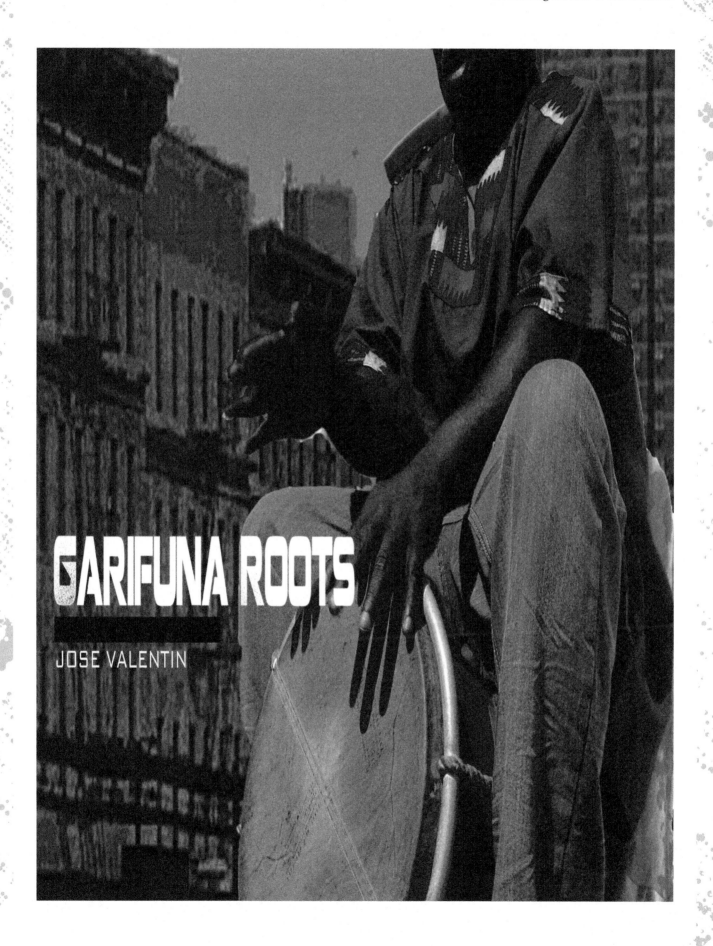

GARIFUNA ROOTS

JOSE VALENTIN

Garifuna Warrior

Forefather prepped, educated for defense of all,

Sensitive in defense of Garifuna without fear or fall,

Traveling at 200 mph wasting no time on pettiness,

Agenda calls for pure, truth, and dignified steadiness,

Sheer knowledge of past and present, unafraid to apply,

Infuriated during disrespect, and immorality to others, simply fly,

Assured words on occasions of threat or tribulation,

Adamant of love for Garifuna with all its foundation,

Always armed for tomorrow, hoping more Garifuna warriors will defend cause.

Forefather driven, it's certain there will never be pause,
For the great Garifuna Warrior will always be!

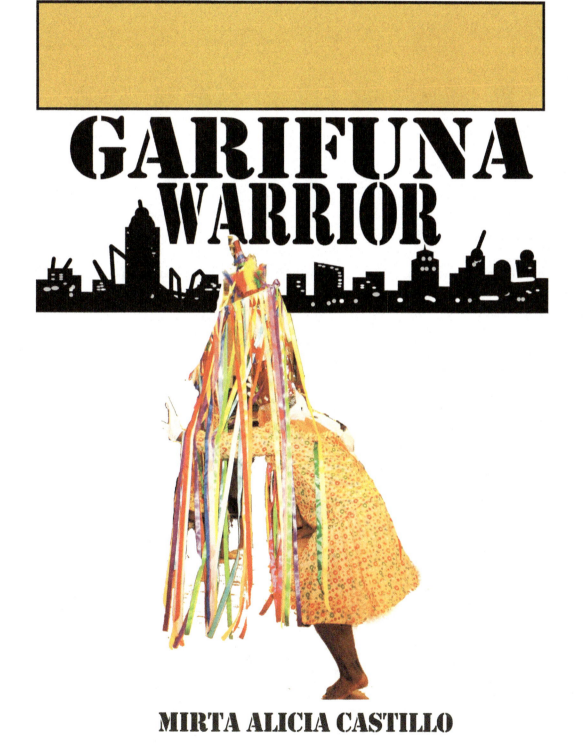

GARIFUNA WARRIOR

MIRTA ALICIA CASTILLO

I Listened

Often asked, "What makes me different?"
For one; I listen.
I can't imagine no stove, no table, no chairs, but this open area is what my ancestors called a kitchen.
Formal education that ends at the fifth grade.
But far more knowledgeable through ancestral stories that never fade.
Passing down clothing to younger siblings.
Made it each day without an adequate standard of living.
Raising malnourished children.
My family passes these stories onto me.
Telling me to be grateful of the opportunities set before me.
Being Garifuna is something I will always be proud to be.
There will always be obstacles in the way.
I have it harder than my ancestors is something I will never say.
I see and hear many of my peers being deported.
I can only wonder if they didn't care of the past struggles or if the message in the stories were distorted.
Garinagu stories provided me with wisdom.
Since day one; I listened.

I Listened

Jose Valentin

The Garifuna In Me

Loving the Garifuna in me
Only Garifuna make me whole
Entrusting all, never of betrayal
Major fowl-up, still owning my goal
Free spirited, guided, excelling
Loving passionately for life is one
Intense love received, and freely I give
Stride sure, no faltering ever allowed
Knees buckle, support is near
The One living in me, victorious
Open positively minus negatively
Zero tolerance for bull, at any given time
Purposeful, for time is of essence
Never ashamed for I am of the Creator's image
Wear head scarf for my ancestry's pride
I am Garifuna that will never tire out
Only till my Creator says, "Your time is here daughter"
The Garifuna in me is more alive than ever before
This Garifuna is God led and ancestry in tuned
Nothing will quiet the Garifuna living within me
The Garifuna in me lives on!
Letting the world know…

Mirta Alicia Castillo

Ubei Nuyi Nu

Ubei nuyi nü

Chibabeime, aransebeime

Demele nabuseruni, bichigeime nü

Demele basugurün lau abameñon nimichuni

Ubei nuyi nü

Sagu basugurün lau, masi lubuidun lihemeri

Mangídabá lau yudi!

Ubei yudi nü, lun nachuruni, nagurüni ligüngün

Mosu hefe lan buidu luntuma lisemedünu

Liseme üwi nei!!!!

Mirta Alicia Castillo

Journey

It's an amazing journey in which Garifuna travel to get here.

Despite the struggles, some terrorize their own community with fear.

Some give up on life and only live through beer.

Unable to cope with the pressure of converting dreams to reality.

An unfortunate cycle that saddens me.

These lessons have taught me to be the best Garifuna I can be.

I don't speak the language.

It doesn't make me any less.

I write the culture on every application and even carry it on my chest.

I can't judge the negative things my own people do.

All i can do is lend support, and ask, "How can I help you"

I feel it's a start.

Looking down at one another will continue to tear us apart.

JOURNEY

JOSE VALENTIN

Look In The Mirror

Ashamed to claim Garinagu.

Pretend not to be from Hondu.

Sour face when looking at hudutu.

Looking down at the opposite sex.

Believing every Garinagu have the virus.

Assuming every Garinagu is possessed.
Hang with Puerto Ricans.

Hang with Dominicans.

Feeling its the only way one feel able to fit in.

Ridicule traditional wear saying that its African.

Hate propels some to lighten their skin.

Cannot deny what lies within.

Refuse to visit the land of their parents.

I don't care about Garifuna, so I will only speak spanish.

Look at what hate has done.

It has made you despise where you are from.

Ultimately, hating yourself for what you have become.

Jose Valentin

GARIFUNA NUGÜYA

Garifuna is handsome, beautiful, and uniquely different,

Garifuna language exhaled sounding graciously fluent,

Head scarves adorned, past and present collide,

Different colors, sophisticated by the wearer's pride,

Some Garifuna fooled about hair being straight,

Others prefer curly and fake, while natural is the trait,

Gentlemen's defense, devote to family protection,

Women face perfect art of passion, love and affection,

Garifuna nugüya accepting who I am then and now,

Garifuna nugüya appreciating similarities, major woww!

Garifuna nugüya, embracing what God blesses us with,

Moving legacy ahead has been Garifuna's wit,

No culture fill this spirit, because Garifuna Nugüya!

San luagu San (100%)!!!!

Mirta Alicia Castillo

Garifuna Soul

I hear desperation at the claim of abandonment,
Hoping someone is considerate of loss and discontentment,

Gloomy days harbor as you discover your own being distant,
None like the ancestral ones who are no longer existent,

Who will you embody now?
While more than few don't want anything with thou,
While to the white man they bow,

Long for companionship, spirit, mind and becoming with you, one
Garifuna soul is the missing ingredient that cannot be outdone,

Garifuna people, failed at figuring out sense of belonging,
When all they need to do is accept you and quit prolonging,

Do they not know this is the missing link?
So that everything settles and is in sync,

Garifuna soul I welcome thee,
You became sole reason for my jubilee!

Mirta Alicia Castillo

I Am Garifuna

Informed at birth, knowing no other culture, I became,
Eating foods blessed by earth, serve by the most dear,

Language introduction……………………Garifuna
Forcefully learning another man's language to "progress"

Never understood Garifuna's unworthiness towards "progression"
Garifuna a non-progressive language? What? Who determined that?

Moving along as Catholic, Christian, Garifuna? Confusing only if I let it,
Clear as day, there is only one God,

As well as there is one Garifuna being within me,
Being Garifuna, Christ-like is God's aim in my life, respect that if you dare,

Garifuna hair, natural beauty grandmother had with loads of length and tenacity,
No imitation of white, yellow colored's hair textures that most long to become,

Adequate timing to chop off all processes to find Garifuna beauty within,
Scarf tied to head or waistline, either way, tactfully Garifuna,

Swaying to Punta rhythms until hips can't no more,
Flourishing physical aspects, flourishing beauty, flourishing wisdom,

Poorness over greed, humbleness over boastfulness,
Garifuna endeavored to change course and image of tomorrow,

May not be the "original" Garifuna as yesterday's beauties,
Children growing as spitting image of our Garifuna being, carrying us to the next phase,

As I tried to find self, I am beautiful, as I tried to wannabe, I remained beautiful, as I became natural, I am even
more gorgeously Garifuna!

Grateful for the well-roundedness of my world, and my perception,
My world is being the best loving example of Garifuna that I can be!

Mirta Alicia Castillo

Back Home

A bit sad that I can't call it my own.

Same place; different sound.

I can't help but take notice of the changes made from the day I left till now.

Its much livelier.

I wish the changes were made much prior.

Now I am a stranger.

Emotions mixed with happiness and anger.

I never thought I feel this way.

I wish I had the option to stay.

But financially, I like many others were
pushed away.

Content with the improvements.

Just wish, I like so many others were the reason developers went through with it.

No longer bitter or upset.

Just expressing how I feel about a home I can't forget.

My letter to Harlem.

Jose Valentin

DECEPTION

As I Drive By

As I drive by, I leave memories and reminiscence of what used to be,
As I drive by, I hesitate slowing down at stomping grounds that once stumbled over me,

As I drive by, with a heavy heart, I still can't dislike you, God won't allow me to,
As I drive by, not even bad memory of foul words piercing my soul or shunning my spirit will stop me now,

As I drive by, I see a broader horizon, promising tomorrow to be full of blessings and brightness,
As I drive by, red lights will stall my journey, as I catch my breath absorbing the beauty lying ahead,

As I drive by, green lights signal realistic goals, finally reaching my highest potentials,
As I drive by, I collect belongings and still I am steadfast without faltering, because this one is definitely your shortcoming,

As I drive by, I am now left alone to embrace, love and protect myself,
As I drive by, I envision love's intent and blessings through the clouds created, just for me!

As I DRive By

MIRTA ALICIA CASTILLO

Broken Hearted Mistress

Worse than an instantaneous dismiss,

You are in dismay as information is revealed,

Received ring prepared to be queen,

Devastated to an immediate demotion of what could have been,

Finding out brought you tears overwhelming quake as lava prepares for an eruption of fears,

Uncontrolled nerves of what might have been versus deception of the man you claim to love,

Little did you know that your king became the greatest king of dogs,

Married, did you say?

What part did you not understand Ms?

 I am the wife,

Enthroned with multiple darts aimed at my heart,

Wondering who pulled my life apart sending mixed emotions,

My family and life in disarray,

It's not even worth fighting for,

That, I am tired of doing,

You want him, keep him!

All there is left to say to you is, thank you

Dear Broken Hearted Mistress

Broken
Hearted
Mistress

Mirta Alicia Castillo

Conniving

You have the nerve to blatantly create lies,
Without blinking, looking directly into other folk's eyes,

You were expert to toy with feelings not your own,
Without remorse, gladly I am now quick to disown,

Though I think of many things to throw,
I always choose the lady before putting on that show,

A coward you turned out to be,
Mere chance of having to explain make you flee,

Signs of immaturity, failing big time to even fix,
Who will now tolerate your conniving ways?

Quickly realizing that it is one that easily lays,

This is definitely you,

She has always been your perfect boo!

Tear Not My Heart Into Pieces

What? Love, I gave it my all!

Never really worried about love in return,

Imagined it to be automatic, I give, you give,

As I loved, my heart bore it all , so I thought,

Love conquers all, they said,

Was I so caught up in that blind love?

Tear not my heart into pieces, I begged,

What did you see as rose petals remained opened?

Received bits offered, to me then, it was sufficient,
When did I learn to settle for less?

Tear not my heart into pieces, I begged,

Arguments, secrets, no right to know, ruled fiercely,

Oceans of tears drowned me, no rescuer in sight,

Hoped for an interpreter, a mind-reader maybe,

Anyone to dissect quadrants of the heart, to see this pain,

Picked the one whom I shared all with, failed me,

Where were you? What distracted you? I sunk,

Tear not my heart into pieces, I begged,

Wrongdoing outdid the greatest love I once felt,

One-sided love tore my heart into pieces!

Mirta Alicia Castillo

Tear Not My Heart Into Pieces

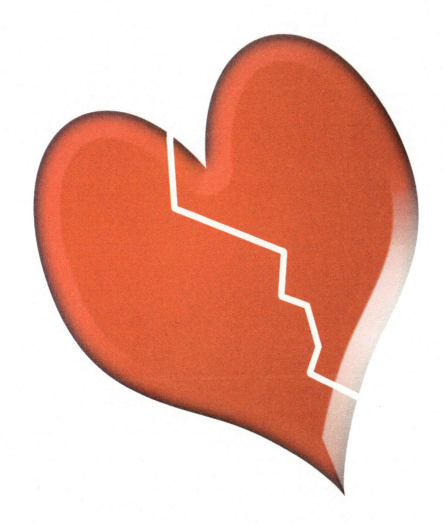

MIRTA ALICIA CASTILLO

DISCRIMINATION

Black With a Spanish Name

They say I'm black with a Spanish name.

I live life through hunger and pain.

Pigmentation remains the same.

Trying to place me in a box, how can society be so vain?

I know where I fit.

The label doesn't exist.

I'm a Garifuna child.

Temperament mild; but my determination is wild.

I'm walking down a journey.

I want to thank my ancestors for the shipwreck set before me.

Passing down strength and power.

Appreciating every second, every minute, and every hour.

Dark in skin, but always Garifuna within.

A very important day.

Let's take a moment and pray for those who sacrificed for what we know as Garifuna settlement day.

Black
with a spanish name.

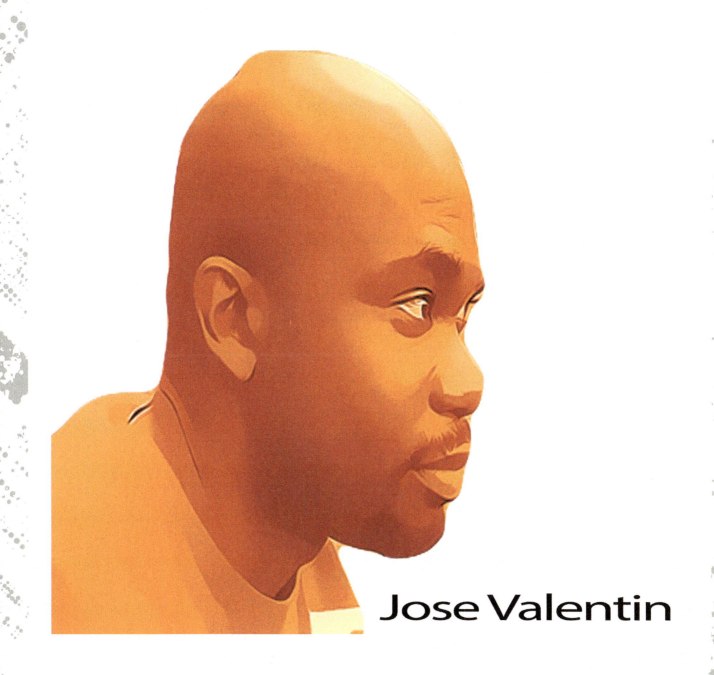

Jose Valentin

Can You Hear Me

I like many others were born in trap.

Targeted Residents Accustomed to Poverty.

Or Targeted Residents Accustomed to Politics.

It took me awhile to acknowledge it.

Looked at the school and prison system and realized how far college is.

Surrounded by swat, marshals, narcs, and detectives.

Looking for fugitives and waking up many families before breakfast.

Families happy the first week of the month.

Depressed for the next few weeks wondering If they have enough.

Profiled as the only group asking for handouts.

In a world full of bigotry and oppression, they are the ones that stand out.

A newly elected president.

Gave some reason to ask, "you voted for him because he's black?"

Now race becomes more prevalent.

Wrongful convictions.

Corrupt politicians.

Sad part of urban living.

Can you hear me??

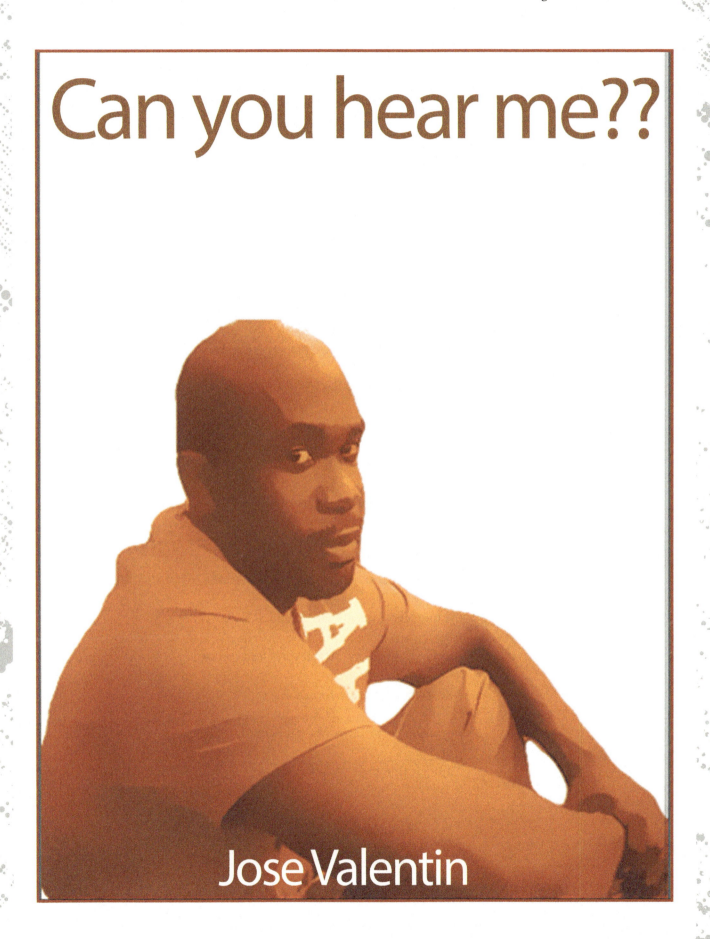

Jose Valentin

Remaining Steadfast

My time to shine shall come

When I do, you will become numb

You can't stand it, through all I remain

Your focus is a knock-out and a sustain

Your heart hateful of substance named melanin

Substance only the Almighty has the power to explain

You may get away stopping shows, never my parade

As I succeed you wish for a masquerade

You hate me, I love you, opposites should attract

But as always your aim is for the ultimate attack

Quit what you do best, while you are still ahead

For the one who rules all will defend as said

Don't touch God's property, all evil ways lead to rest

Take chance and perform the test

You will share stories as you flabbergast

I am left to remain steadfast at last!

Mirta Alicia Castillo

Thanks For Dreaming

Thank you for dreaming.

Thank you for dreaming about equality.

We still have more steps but we are working towards making your dream a reality.

You may be a bit disappointed because there are still many living in poverty.

There is also a new indestructible version of slavery.

Some call it prison and some call it the penitentiary.

Where fathers get locked up and become a distant memory.

Children grow up and look upon each other as their mortal enemy.

Many have spoken that we need a new leader.

But the problem is that we have become fewer readers.

Less read books that can enlighten us.

We slowly began losing the fight in us.

The media continues to tell lies to our vision.

Bigots continue to hide behind religion.

Thank you for helping create our civil rights.

You are the reason I write.

The reason I fight against prejudices and stereotypes.

It took many years to have you honored for a holiday.

I like many others admire and respect you every day.

Jose Valentin

Thoughts

I see many walking around with a blank stare.

Hopelessness has many protesting to show America that corruption stops here.

Cynicism knows that such a thing won't disappear.

More robberies; more homicides.

Using violence as a way to cope with the hunger inside.

8 years of damage.

Still they blame a recently elected president; I can't understand it.

Jim Crow states locking up those whose first language is Spanish.

"Send them back", they're all illegal.

I thought under god we were all considered equal.

Some say I'm not black enough.

To some I will be validated if I sit in a back of a car with cuffs.

Literacy rate continue to go downhill.

To many focused on making that first mil.

Human compassion continues to lack..

Lack of education and too much pigmentation can hold you back, an unfortunate fact.

Praised for going in the system.

Less acknowledge for refined wisdom.

Means mugs instead of hugs.

I killed that N???a just because.

This is what self-esteem does.

Replaces love with hate.

We are killing ourselves at a uncontrollable rate.

I can only continue to pray to god but, by then, it may be too late.

Jose Valentin

Unequal

So many years of oppression.

Many, question the votes of the people of color during the last election.

Fearing hope and change becoming the new direction.

The President's birth certificate became the hot question.

The Tea party became the new movement.

Some claim racism is over but the party has shown that's far from proven.

You voted for the President because he's black, right?

I voted for him because it seemed right.

He's passionate, articulate, and amazingly bright.

If you weren't so ignorant, you would realize that he's half white.

The type of ignorance people often face.

Not so openly discussed because we supposedly live in a world where we are open to race.

I embrace who I am.

I will continue to defend my people.

I will continue to defend those who are considered unequal.

 Its been overturned but we unfortunately live in a world that is still separate and unequal.

 Jose Valentin

Who Am I?

I am monitored as I walk through a store.

Often told to place on my hands up on the wall.

People automatically assume I'm poor.

I get paid a lower wage.

I am only respected while on stage.

Occasionally admired for being a hero when I'm on the front page.

I am a nanny to non-biological children.

While my kids live in horrible conditions.

I am fatherless.

The profitable institution is part of this.

I am surrounded by drug addicts.

It took me a long time to acknowledge it.

The portrayal of who am I is distorted through media and politics.

Some of my peers are killed over sneakers.

Where is the media coverage of inspirational teachers?

We are only good at sports.

Many achievements receive negative feedback.

One sided view to who am I.

Jose Valentin

DON'T GET IT TWISTED!

Do Me Right

Walking off again, oh my! How I despise it so!

I wanted it to work this time, love is all I search for, over and over again!

Men, oh my men, I want you to...understand me.

I am a woman in need of...feeling loved, caressed, vibrant, and can't you see it in my eyes?...Mellow, Aching and longing desire of seduction at the mere presence of you.

See how my eyes communicate in response to your touch...reach, reach for my...spirit and the joy I feel when you treat me like a queen.

You hardly give it to me...the respect that I duly deserve, I am so, but so craving it...please share it with me, will you feed it to me?.... The stories I long to hear, about your upbringing and how you came to be.

Hold it, grab it baby...the feelings that destroy my insides as you pivot to walk off after the hurt you left behind.

Allow me to whisper these words into your ears, I love you, did you hear me? I love you...but if you are going to keep it up, I will always choose me over you!

DO
ME
RIGHT
MIRTA ALICIA CASTILLO

I OWE IT TO MYSELF

Making parents proud of all lessons taught, I owe it to myself,

Respecting their wish, by carefully following directives, I owe it to myself,

Reminiscent of days restricted from hang out with friends, I owe it to myself,

To give respect and receive respect in return, I owe it to myself,

Where no man was good enough for me, only a king, I owe it to myself,

Grabbing all positive endeavors, minimizing negatives,

Loving endlessly whether it's an enemy or a neighbor, I owe it to myself,

When fowling up, without self-beating, picking myself up quickly, moving along
I owe it to myself,

To live life to the fullest without circumstantial drama, I owe it to myself,

To jump into the unknown with intimate confidence knowing I will be fine,
I owe it to myself,

Loving all of me, and being thankful to every being that made me,
I owe it to myself,

To share abundant love embedded in my being, I owe to myself,

To let loose the Garifuna in me to embrace all attributes granted by the Most High,
I owe it to myself,

To be different and make a difference in the lives of all, surrounding me,
I owe it to myself,

To find love in the crevices of the earth where that man would be different, kind, loving, and only for me!

I owe that much to myself, no more settling for less!

I owe it to myself

MIRTA ALICIA CASTILLO

Women Bloom Like Flowers

Loving days, great sunshine, and warm weather opens us to receive the greatest love of all,

Spiritually in tuned, negativity bouncing off, just like bad weather, beating upon the most beautiful flower and yet it stands, looking even more beautiful after the storm,

Whichever way we are abandoned, leave us alone, leave us outside if you have to, so that the ray of light shine upon us, so the rain wash away all that causes withering,

The least you can do for us is leaving us outside under the care of the Almighty to repair damages,

God shelters all abandoned, restoring it by giving clarity of light, tranquility, nourishment, and tender loving care,

Abandoned, God allow someone else to pass us by, look at us, admire our beauty, and take us in, to take better care of us,

Taking time to detoxify, prepare us to love again, done right, we give our all, we blossom in beauty giving the most radiant smiles, capturing the attraction from many others, great sign that God was in the midst of repairing all wrongfully done by men who did not appreciate the beautiful flower they had in their grasp,

Ironically, most of our problems are either worsened or repaired by the introduction of another flower into the frame,

God takes care of his flowers just as he did in his most beautiful Garden of Eden ever known to mankind, keeping us beautiful, melting our hearts into our caring ways, radiant, peaceful, and most importantly, listening to all we have to share with him, word for word.

Under His care we are better equipped to face the biggest challenges that many of our men falter or lack,

Feel not offended gentlemen, for there are many flowers deserving the best care you may not be equipped to give, simply walk on by, for the thorns may hurt you!

Women Bloom Like Flowers
MIRTA ALICIA CASTILLO

You Aught Not Be Fooled!

You aught not be fooled if you are to abhor my facial characteristics,
You will notice "improvement" being part of your foolish statistics,

You aught not be fooled of the beauty designed by the image of God,
So, who are you to frown, look down, or sneer upon me, and think I'm odd,

You aught not be fooled by the color God deemed appropriate for me,
May possibly be the same reason he made the planets, men/women, and thee,

You aught not be fooled of the knowledge whirling in my brain,
It should suffice, features are same, because of the one who Reigns,

You aught not be fooled of the progress and opportunity given to us,
Because you will be highly disappointed of the results, and it is just!

You aught not be fooled of our opportunities at progression,
As the 45th President of U.S.A becomes the essence of a re-election,

You aught not be fooled for there was once a dream enriched with revelations,
To your surprise, it is impressive that on the same day, it became double celebrations,

You aught not be fooled, as you scheme & find ways to keep us oppressed,
There is One that will always rise to the occasion, and it will be addressed!
You Aught Not Be Fooled!

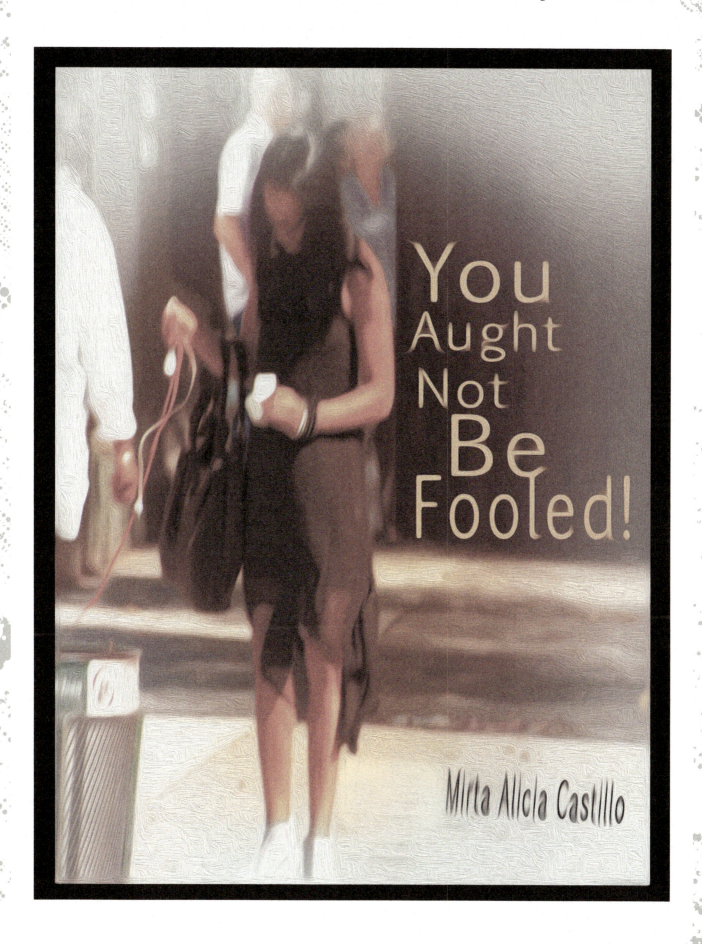

You
Aught
Not
Be
Fooled!

Mirta Alicia Castillo

Catch Me While I'm asleep

People may say I'm bizarre,

Treasuring this mind and heart is my duty thus far,

Numbness similarly to sleep is how I used to deal,

Cognition remain intact, self let-down is no more, for real!

Comatose maybe, will I revert, even then, prefer 6 ft under,

Living to defend acquired knowledge, like rolling thunder,

While I'm awake, I see, hear, taste, feel, therefore I am alive,

I defend everything related to me, so this is how I thrive,

Catch me while I am sleeping, it's the only way you'll get away!

Just hope, I don't quickly snap out of my sleep!

Mirta Alicia Castillo

My Power Shrinks

My power shrinks as we argue, fuss, and fight,
Don't you realize I wasn't made to be that type?

You work against God's plans, I know that he dictates how I should be taken care of,
Peace is my most familiar place, communication, my savior!

Allow me to live peaceful, think prosperous, for our tomorrow,
Many problems between us take away the sweetness leaving bitterness,

Do you not see? The better you treat me, the more loving you receive!
Study me as your partner; wouldn't you want what's best?

Don't tear my heart into pieces, stop and reflect,
The more you hurt me, the more you park yourself on the curve,
Bringing this relationship to a quick halt,

As you continue treating me and others this way, you will find yourself by yourself!
No more fights, arguments, or fussing, allow love, peace and understanding take its course,

For I too want this love to dwell forever,
Uplifting my strength to the opposite direction, just as God intended,

Lift me to higher grounds, and I will lift you!

Mirta Alicia Castillo

Tried My Best Not To Compare

Good men have become yet so scarce,
Men gather hearing the same story to share,

Machismo, here and machismo there,
All there is to say is, oh dear!

Inquiring about my past life, expectant and anticipating different,
Instead it turned sour, throwing stories back in my face,

Obtaining info, as if life would now be smooth-sailing,
Disappointed to discover, another whirlwind of troubles,

Forgetting that machismo in my community is alive,
In whose mind does it fit wanting to control someone else?

One's own life spins out of control, to be managing someone else's,
Machismo grew old and does not work within this generation,

Get with the program, let ladies breathe, and be themselves,
You will have a much healthier relationship, Garifuna gentleman!

Loosen your grip; life is hard as it is,
Give love, and understanding, not machismo!

Well, you can't say, I didn't try my best not to compare!

Mirta Alicia Castillo

LOVE

Baby You Make Me Feel

Where did these butterflies come from as I see you?

A wind of cool refreshing air entering every part of my being,

Your gaze warm, one my heart desired to beat rhythmically,

Racing to a different beat, of goodness, kindness and real love,

Afraid of taking steps, drawing me closer to what I imagined from afar,

Anxious and fear of confronting this reality, called you,

Proximity causing hand clamminess, eyes widening to absorb the moment,

Spitting image of handsomeness to be taken in slowly,

Conversations, seeing you, holding me or my hand, no longer seem sufficient,

Sudden addiction and rush became overwhelming, calmed by your presence,

True love maybe, one thing certain, this sensation requires exploring,

Exploring I went, the deeper I dug, the sweeter it got, oh my what is this?

You keep me in love, with all purity offered,

You deserve love in return for mastering how to talk, love, and respect me

Baby you make me feel......!!!!

Baby You Make Me Feel!

Mirta Alicia Castillo

Don't Forget The Hugs

Hugs comfort,
In good and bad times, even as I hurt,

Hugs reassure,
As the heat from body temperature,

Hugs affirm,
Given and received to make me squirm,

Hugs are everlasting,
Hold me longer for I am panting,

Hugs are yearned,
Always willing, and I have learned,

Feeling lonely, hugs this good should be shared with pureness,
Withhold not the yearning of love and closeness,
Show me warmth and that of kindness,

Give hugs willingly; you will always receive in return,

The one who lacked hugs, will be the one who values it most!

Don't forget the hugs!

Don't Forget the Hugs

MIRTA ALICIA CASTILLO

Hush Baby

Things turn sour in a split second,
Just when things were just friendly,

How did that happen?
Where did we go wrong?

You are certainly mistaken,
Hush baby, allow me to rub your back,
I think bare skin rub is your preference?

Hush baby, you still talking?
A caress at the nape of your neck,

Did you just stutter babe?
Woah! Huh? Can't understand you, ok babe,

Quieting you, will require bringing it lower,
Hush baby, bare chest, lower did you say?

Hard or soft rub babe? Don't answer that!
This must remain clean for my readers, hush baby!

Hush Baby

Mirta Alicia Castillo

I Love You

I love you now, as I loved you then,

Today is a replica of yesterday,

As we flow and surpass decades of immense joy,

Cover me with hugs and kisses, nobody has ever planted on me before,

No wonder I no longer know how to act,

Love from you cannot be replaced by any other in my lifetime,

Oh and I keep feeling, all the time, dumbfounded,

Relying on each other, we are the best things God created,

Once and for all, we remain deeply profound.

Eternal love I see no other,

Words cannot express the admiration and continued spunk,

And the enticing love I feel for you

Honey, I love you!

Mirta Alicia Castillo

It's Gotta Feel Right!

Everyone think there is time constraint for being alone,

Must rush into something new, at least they say,

Though missing the company, fear of loneliness lurks,

Sensation compressed of vivid repetition of yesterday's chaos,

Never imagined something like that would happen,

With parents setting the example, who would have imagined?

Living day by day with God's guidance is what I aspire,

I am never alone, not rushing to undo peace of mind I now have,

I will wait until things feels right, heaven sent, that's all!

Its got to feel right, if it does not, it's a no go.

Guidance from above, everything is alright, so I patiently wait
for the clear sign,

This time around, It's Gotta Feel Right!

Kisses Galore

Starting with a tap kiss,

Sending me to a quick bliss,

Second tap tasting sweeter,

Partitioning lips never felt better,

Partition and draw close and closer, oh how sweet!

Flavorful mint chocolates, caramel, wow such heat!

Biting softly unable to come to a sudden stop,

Flying high never coming down from the mountain top,

Woah, Woah, I think it's time to take it easy,

With so many kisses, I am feeling queasy,

I am asking you for more kisses plant them galore!

Making sure I don't forget, I beg, bring it to the core!

Kisses Galore

MIRTA ALICIA CASTILLO

Lend me

I'm not always going to need your expertise for repair,

Exceptional times during loneliness while in despair,

Lend me love that is easily shared truly, from the heart,

Invoke powerful words, snap me out of desperation without feeling apart,

Utter all that is always derived from above,

Refer me to soul searching scripture, enabler of all love,

Emotion, an unannounced eruptive tidal wave at its peak,

Embarrassedly aiming control, too late, it is you I seek,

Damaged outcome, drowning, reaching arms high, you rescue,

Easily lend yourself for me to hold, ease nerves, calming fear is queue,

Secure your grip just a little while, don't let go,

Wipe away the tears, until there is none left but a glow,

Thanks for reassurance, although familiar to me, feels great to hear it again,

Lend me, simply because you are for me today, and I for you tomorrow just as He ordains!

MIRTA ALICIA CASTILLO

LETTING LOVE FLOURISH

Sweetheart, I love the experience my heart settles
into, it seems,

Scary are these moments because I don't ever want to
change the fantasy of these scenes,

Smile never seem wider, for this pleasure can become
obscene,

Beautiful and certain that its emotion shared
amongst us two,

Treasure me, as I will you,

Uplifting desire rumbling through our bodies,

Unique feelings never felt before, we easily let go smoothly,

This couldn't feel wrong for I use God as guide,

First time around, inexperienced and got tried,

Spirit led in every way, letting love flourish,

Happiness bound with spirit free flowing, while you
nourish,

No settling for less, for God always bless best!

Letting Love Flourish

MIRTA ALICIA CASTILLO

Loving Again

Loving again, everything seems insane.
Familiar place, same gender, same loving feeling at the start of it all, should I just abstain?

Not fair to treat people the same, when they may be different, but what a gamble it is!
Glancing here and glancing there, I see all these cuties.

There is one who holds my heart fonder causing all kinds of irregularities.
Can't resist, will I be faced with another actor?

It is clear, meant to receive love and give in return.
I must learn again not to be so stern.

Pain aimed at killing all beauty, while true love resuscitates.
Breath of fresh air through my lung as it penetrates.

Rejuvenating skin so, it is thought I bleach.
Stride now so sure I teach.

Composure intact even the boldest dare not mess with me. Don't want to be a drill sergeant, Just seeking true love.

Free as a butterfly learning to use its broken wing again.
Taking in all wind and all freedom.

Triumphant and assured true love will forever reign.
Love never failing lurking in many different ways!

Gently I give in to the one worthy of embellishing all of God's property!

Loving Again

Mirta Alicia Castillo

Love Expectations

Love me at my highest and at my lowest,
Tire not of the excess at either extreme,

Be patient enough to hold me through it all,
Certain of the needed and most wanted desires,

Now more than ever sure of what I search for,
I'm not searching for life I exited from, hell no!

Listen to all my concerns as I will do yours,
Even if you miss one or two from the many I will have,

Rub my back and I will rub yours, warmness is my tee,
Return the sparkling look of love in my eyes,

Plant the kiss sending shivers of thrill throughout,
Heal me with addicting tender touch aching for more,

Teach me that one to one love exist on planet earth,
Failed at sharing in kindergarten, why will I pass now?

Love me tenderly to regain strong hold of passion,
Hold my hands secure, assure your strong grip,

Never letting go, as I may attempt in stepping away,
Fear may drive me away, but hold on to me,

I may head for the escape, because of uncertainty,
Pull me closer to take in the sweetest scent of you,

Know you are nearer and feeling you closer now,
As I lay cover me with the highest love expectations,

You will know you are a keeper as I crave for more!

MIRTA ALICIA CASTILLO

Love Expectations

Loving You My Way

Frightening enough, love terminated all fears,
Lonely place, even accompanied by many years,

Controllably I love now, when before, I didn't respect
caution,
Gave it my all, as long as I was with self-satisfaction,

Primarily concerned about my contribution, as time
was of essence no one was there for me,
The shoulder I longed for was scarce, there was
nothing left, all there was left was to flee,

Now free to love my way, take it or leave it, choice is
now yours
New boo in my life, I will love my way, show me how you love, so I won't show you no doors,

Loving your way is not ideal till you have passed the test of time,
In the meantime, hold me close don't let go just till I'm sure you are mine

I will let you lead when you show me true magic,
Hold my hands and show the world the beauty of your queen so that it does not become tragic,

You would have succeeded when you lift me higher than the place I once stood,
Allowing confidence to return the way It originally should,

Loving you my way, is what I long for if you must insist,
If it come down to nitty gritty I will never resist,

I will always love you from now on, my way!

Who Loves You Baby?

I Love you, simply for being you,

I Love you, when you are feeling blue,

I Love you, when I see you struggling with fears,

I Love you, when your sensitivity bring great tears,

I Love you, when uncertainty dwells in your heart,

I Love you, when drawing yourself far apart,

I Love you, because despite all, you don't falter,

I Love you, because you didn't drown underwater,

I Love you through all of the grief you encounter,

I Love you, even when people don't see when they
are bringing you to a downer,

I Love you when things feel as if nothing is ever going right

I've learned to love me more now, as I defeat all fight,

Who else accept flaws to allow growth and maturity?

Had I avoided weakness I would've remained in obscurity,

In tune with weakness, can relate and help someone through theirs,

I Love you through life's course of negativity as I have been granted heirs,

One that conquer weakness has conquered laws of survival of most fittest,

I Love you because the greatest love is that from the most Highest,

I Love more the one who dwells in me, sustaining, and renewing our spirits every day.

God loves you baby!

Who ❤'s you Baby?

MIRTA ALICIA CASTILLO

You are simply Amazing!

Treasuring every moment spent with you,

Every I love you, every whisper sending special waves of desire unfamiliar to me,

A touch so gentle, awakening the innermost part of me,

Lip quivering aiming never to pull away from the warmth of your kiss,

Hugs feeling so desirably secure, I beg you never let go,

Hold me tight, never release the grip,

Never let go this beautiful thing called "real love"

Real love that cries, holds, comfort, grows, supports, loving in every given opportunity,

Repeatedly you make me yearn for you day in and day out, bringing it to the next level,

You are simply amazing!

You Are Simply Amazing!

MIRTA ALICIA CASTILLO

Virginia Johns   Tri-Shone Randall

Embrace Me

Desperate for your embrace,
Send me not on a goose chase,

Whether things are good or bad, embrace me,
Let it feel homely, I will forever remain here,

Love me despite arguments and fights alike,
Is it that serious?

Embrace my sorrows, and vile memory of yesterday,
Every willing embrace, brings me home,

My definite fixer-upper,
Dependent on the embrace that will always catch me,

Before that hard thump unto the ground,
Your strength and the little bit of mine, sustains me,

Hold me, never let go!
Hold me closer and tighter, never pushing me away,

Squeeze me as a sponge, pushing old out and all new in,
New love, desire, and hope, embrace me now, until forever!

Mirta Alicia Castillo

IN AWE OF YOU!

Not believing at times,
Seeming untrue, most times,

A special someone wanting me?
Who alerted you to choose me?

Choosing me out of the crowd, wow tasking!
Your stare pierce my soul, burning,

Loving eyes melt me into pieces,
Every gaze your way, it gradually increases,

Oooh baby don't do that, shift your gaze!
Looking behind me in case it's a mistake,

Oh yeah, it is me, can't no longer help it
Loving every moment of this!

You not bad at all, hmmm scent driven wildness,
Never before conscious of features, now a must!

No doubt, loving what I perceive, ouch baby!
Biting lower lips as you stare it down,

Careful babes, it may just go down, just like that!

In awe of you!

Mirta Alicia Castillo

Is This love That I'm feeling?

Love blooms at unknown times, and how it all occurs, who knows?

Saying no, it's like admitting a yes, yet so confusing, what a blur!

Check marks in place, behavioral outbursts, dictatorship, oooh scary!

Love, patient as it seems, listens, holds, senses, supports, how contrary!

It is not what you have in your mind alone, aiming to change me?

Me, who have been reared by two, knowing the difference, me?

No more of that; you say, I say, we both say as we define compromise,

Butterflies, ooooh yeah, sweetest sensation wishing never to demise,

Loudest, sweetest music ever heard, playing over and over in my head,

Blowing wind never felt refreshing and welcomed, desiring now to wed,

Uttering words into my ears, tickling my fancy,

Such high, a familiar place I never should have fallen off of and now I chancy,

Unsure of what may come, hold me tight, better yet squeeze me tight, till I decide,

Plant those kisses that sends me spinning into confusion, just until it subsides,

As we groove into Bob Marley's song "Is this Love That I'm Feeling?"

Groove me as you know how, grinding and swaying for I know this by heart.

Take me there daddy!

Mirta Alicia Castillo

Loving Me

Best inheritance granted from the One above,
Can't disappoint Him because within me He interwove,

Internal love, humanity can't touch, as all else bombards,
Even as I confront the worst climactic blizzards,

Loving God who loved me first,
Beautiful patterned life, all should equip thy self,

Loving me through this storm called life,
Stages spring-up, as attitude determines level of strife,

As I am challenged, thank God I know and love me,
For I feel sorry for those coming blindly,

Loving me keeps me controlled,
Allowing the Most High in life to always remain enrolled,

Loving me, serves as a reminder that He first loved me,
My soul's secret to never stopping this wonderful sensation of, Loving Me!

Mirta Alicia Castillo

Loving Strength

Love given is love received,

Two joining, and sustains longevity,

Keeps the heart fond with memorabilia,

Great love supports understanding,

Love touches the innermost sensitive parts,

Provided by one is sufficient enough,

More than one is prohibited and forbidden,

Given correctly it flushes and flourishes,

Loving strength is all I pursue to push ahead,

If ever you are not willing to give it,

Always revert back for the best loving strength embedded,

Internally for this Garifuna...

Mirta Alicia Castillo

Pamper Me

Hold me in my despair,
Hold me even when all is unfair,

Kiss me until I am wanting,
Kiss me just until there is panting,

Whisper softly as I engage in your warmth,
Whisper softly until you get the response you want,

Rub my back, so that I squirm closer to you,
Rub my back, until we both have the queue,

Arouse that part of me that has been dormant,
Close off all memory that tends to bring torment,

Pamper me, for I will pamper you,
Pamper me anytime for I won't complain,

Define pampering as the sweetest taboo of your wildest desires!

Mirta Alicia Castillo

There is Something Different About You

There is something different about you,
There is a saying that not every guy is same,
From the first day I confirmed the instant flame,

Penetrating stare burned my soul,
Warmth confirmed my heart stolen whole,

Touching my face sending sparks flying,

Who asked you to do that without me stricking?

Instead a wave of intensity begin overwhelming as I melt
Overwhelming goodness, never previously felt,

Any other time I would have struck, woah, woah, what a kiss!
Do it again, so I can confirm it and not consider it a diss,

You are here now, our closeness speak louder than words ever would,
Oh how I desire this feeling to never leave, for internally it feels good,

You want what I want, and I want what you want, that's the challenge!

Rare occurrence of perfection, let's aim for the plunge!

Mirta Alicia Castillo

You Compliment Me

You make me smile, you deserve my widest smiles,

You say the sweetest things; the aim is getting to the extra miles,

You shift calamities to calmness, making me temperate,

You provide warmth at which times I feel desperate,

You protect me; this is why I don't ever mind being "covered" like Gregory Isaacs,

You compliment me; this is why we are where we are, passed basics!

Mirta Alicia Castillo

OUTLOOK TO LIFE/FUTURE

Always Have My Back

Wholesome in spirit, mind, body, and soul,

In sync throughout, now I see control,

Thanks for lengthy talks, just when I didn't see beyond,

Painted the most beautiful picture of what was to have dawned,

Falling backwards, knowing you are there to grab and hold,

"You are special", you'd say, when it was you all along,

Blessed am I having that special someone to tell me I belong,

Few people live this in their lifetime, blessed with great love and support,

Count on me for I too will scratch your back as you have mine,

Even the silence of the moments are understood, a quick fix by a wine and dine,

You have no idea of your worth, now you are in my heart to abide,

I will always have your back, for through my worst you rode,

Thank God, he brought you into my life, just in the nick of time,

For He never fails to safeguard our backs!

Always Have My Back

MIRTA ALICIA CASTILLO

Delicately Unwrapped

Tiniest gift sent from above, unwrapped, delicately

Loving kindness turning frown upside down, intricately

Second I laid eyes on you, precious you already were

More valuable than ruby, gold, and diamonds, yes sir!

Long awaited, best blessing has yet to come

Can't wait to hold the best gift ever granted to some

Thank you Lord, gift is opened gladly with assurance

Unwrapped, yet to perfect fit and deliverance

unbeknownst to you Lord, you sent it unwrapped for it never to be forgotten!

Who is the best gift provider?

Best gift received are unwrapped ones, bammm!!!

In your face!

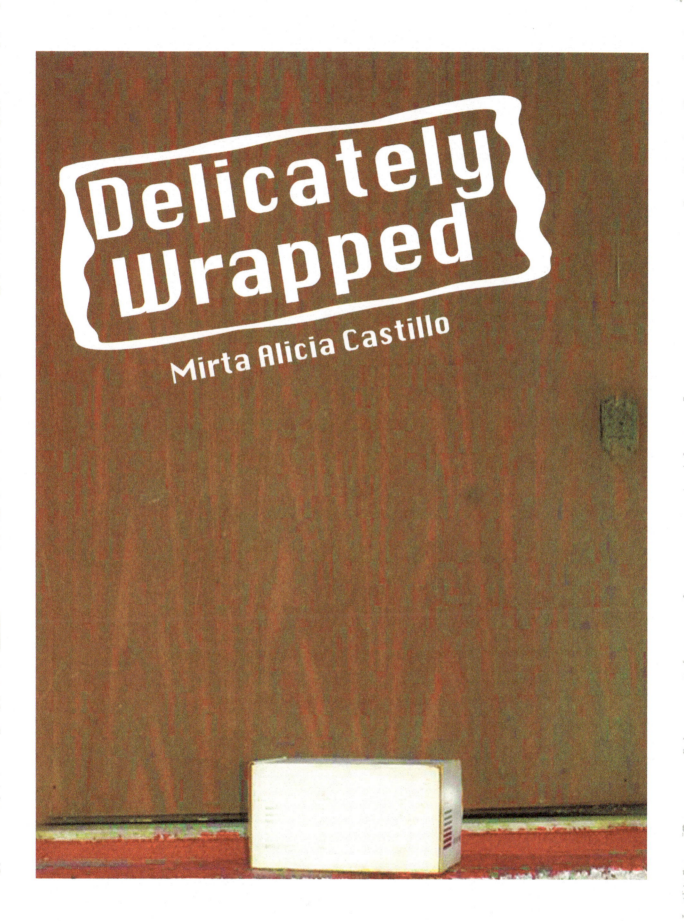

Delicately Wrapped

Mirta Alicia Castillo

Flowing Thru Time Gracefully

I watch you approach, you know what you bring, it
remains a question mark to me,

I don't fret because the one that bring you forth, also
loves me,

Although there were strains, torments, and turmoil, I
remained standing,

Others never imagined my desperate call for
emergency rescue,

Smiling, behind it all served to mask all sufferings,

All came during your time, now you exit, becoming
2011's history,

Thru it all I was challenged, now I am challenging the
upcoming one,

I hold my hips and wait, not afraid of what's to come,

Sensing victory in the making, with peace not too far
behind,

New Year I will embrace you with new beginnings, hope, a
clearer and promising clean start.

No attachments to pull me down, flowing gracefully
through these next month's finally living, doing me,

Flowing thru time gracefully is always God's mercies
poured over me, come what may!

Flowing Through Time Gracefully

MIRTA ALICIA CASTILLO

God's Perfect Timing

When occasionally I doubted,
Tears rolled down my face,
Thought you forgot about my life,
You didn't see life nor joy in mine,
Truthfully enough, neither did I,
My solution, use your gift to fix,
You had plans of your own,
Failing at granting my awaited gift,
Thought life was perfect in mind,
Ideal, had you only listened to me,
Over time I became inconsolable,
As my greatest gift I yearned,
Going through life I saw none else,
Mindfully occupied with topics,
Relationally dealing with my claim,
Emotions and tears drained me,
Where were you? I needed you!
Ok, God I see how difficult life is!
Facilitator, isn't it what you are?
Obvious lesson for me to learn,
So, swiftly I move on, still hoping,
Maybe even pity will succumb,
As tears dried, composure intact,
Peacefully, I asked for forgiveness,
Awaited spiritual redemption,
By my side you were through it all,
Everything was upside down,
Imagined nightmare without you,
As you decided to bless my life,
Knowing I would appreciate more,
When I least expected grace,
Just when I was no longer,
making it my ultimate priority
you showed me, it was always
Not on my timing, but on
God's Perfect Timing!

God's Perfect Timing

Storming Strength

Just when you think I'm weak
Just as you ignore me, thinking to overpower
Just as stepping out, you took a piece of me
Just as tears shed ignited fuel for continuity
Just as lost interest in maintaining our environment
Just as cat caught tongue of endless weeks of silence
Just as the ultimate "I don't have anything to say"
Just as I am going to my "friend's" house
Just as "I'm not hungry, I already ate"
Just as you doll-up to step out
Just as ignorance became your best virtue
Just as foulness took over your language
Just as "Don't publish our joint pictures"
Just as "I pay my phone bill, don't touch my phone"
Just as "I'm on my way, will be there in no time" and the long waits
Just as too many let downs
Just as what do you mean you can't accompany me?
Just as the most difficult moments you faltered to comfort, and to hold
Just as twisted you spun my life, with storming strength I endured
Just as the storm intensified muscles tightened to sprint from destructive emotional toil
Just as I am free I run with storming strength to get me to tomorrow
Just as tomorrow is here, I wouldn't look back to relive the cruelty of yesterday

STORMING STRENGTH

MIRTA ALICIA CASTILLO

The Sun Shall Rise Again

The sun shall rise again,

Observing meadows as dusk set,

Unknown what the night may reveal,

Pitch midnight darkness, confusing directions, poor focus,

Guided by the good feel of this moment,

Unsure of the significance by daybreak, keeping it moving,

Steadfast along this night, hoping all done, may or may not please anyone but me,

Do I run with this feeling? Whether good or bad, I will know when sun rise again,

Asking the one above, my path illuminate, even in physical darkness for light to shine,

The sun shall rise again brightly for me to see all things through a different eye,

Seeing God's wonders even when screwing things up, knowing the sun shall rise again,

I am hopeful!

Mirta Alicia Castillo

Tomorrow's Promise

Living an opportunity yet to come,

Feelings of heaven on earth below,

Blessed to know all is not necessarily discomfort,

Today differ because of excitement's descent,

Encouragement becomes pain's threshold,

Advice clarifying opaque windows of opportunity,

Light beaming brightly at the end of the tunnel,

Cracking a smile is my soul's awakening,

Expressing joyful thanks to my Father above,

Assuring continuation of exhalation,

Believing tomorrow will shine ever so brightly,

Expelling toxic from pores where anguish once dwelled,

Tomorrow's promise sustaining me today,

Hope is my strongest grip, not planning on letting go,

God's reassurance of tomorrow's promise,

Remaining lifted high even when not aware of His divine mercies!

Mirta Alicia Castillo

Amazement

Caught in a web, plotting an exit, can't seem to untangle

Cognizant of my window of opportunity, yet doubt creeps

At times web become astute than faith, but God still comes

He rescues, while in disbelief, at the same time I'm in awe!

It's not in my deceptive time, but God's time

Knocking on unanswered doors, leading to wrong paths I fall

Maybe answered doors were ok temporarily, yet I'm thankful

Despite all, knees remained bent eyes shut, focused, Jesus comforted

All I have to say is my Heavenly Father got this!

God in the midst of things, all is awesome!

Standing ahead of me are my biggest blessings of all time

God you make me feel amazing!

All the anguish, webs, depression was all worthwhile!

Can't imagine my life without you!

Thank you Jesus for you're always my amazement!!!!

Mirta Alicia Castillo

DETERMINED TO MAKE IT

I am going to get there,

Regardless of who may cheer or may even sneer,

I will get there, come what may,

Eager for things to happen right away,

Proving to the world that this feeling I will not shake,

If I let go, uneasiness and regret will overtake,

Jolted battle within; positive attitude, will surely win,

Should've, would've kept at minimum deep within,

I will make it, faith in the most High, already done,

Never ending, never failing, promised to everyone,

As I place my foot forward I do so in confidence,

Knowing destiny waits with open arms in reverence,

Determined To Make It!

Mirta Alicia Castillo

God In My Life

God in my life

My solidarity to God, firm, proven faithful

Popularity is not my aim,

Nor am I searching for fame,

Never ashamed, For God so loved the world

Reigning, love will never be an issue for this pearl

Cheerfully performing and doing good deeds

Fretting not my thing, for He takes care of my needs

Praising Him, I am joyful, for He is a feel good God

Weak times lead to strong times as I smile to a nod

Why not share this great wonder called, God?

Keeping silent of His wonder, is shameful

So I give myself to serve Him for he is worthy and merciful

Devoted until I am called home to be in His presence

Times challenging, I rather God anytime

For He is by my side all the time

Lord I praise you because of who you are!

You are God all by yourself, and I love you, just because!

Mirta Alicia Castillo

Heart, Suffer No More

Rejoice for all has come to an end,

Yesterday's troubles causes no more reason to pretend,

Days of teary-eyes gone, for all there is left, is satisfaction and clarity,

Leaping beats of happiness and laughter, never seeming like peculiarity,

Rhythmic regularity supplying nourishment, calmness, wholesomely,

Became an unfamiliar rhythm for a while, but God restores purely,

Fear no more, for my God is here, was and always will be in control,

You are the reason I live and breathe vitality, allowing all else to roll,

Sacredly Jesus and you are like that hand and glove, fitting to perfection,

Conjunctively easing my stressors, treasuring you have become my satisfaction,

Heart, suffer no more, for from here on, you are priority,

Endurance and longevity depends on the One above, taking care of my sensitivity and spirituality

Heart, suffer no more!

Mirta Alicia Castillo

RELATIONSHIPS

My Dearest Mom

Mother, one most dear,
One who held me during extreme fear,
Embrace warm enough to this day still feel,
Your presence constant as was your love,
Special love only you, dad and your other children knew,
Like a spoiled child, given all life's luxuries in a lump sum, Love you gave, and was felt. Gaze always out-stretched in different directions in lieu of safety,
Proud Garifuna you were, demonstrated how to be proud of my scarf and attire. Never minding to look after your children, you did it with unconditional love,
Caring and loving others without losing your cool nor yourself,
Meal preparations no one to date can top, exquisitely divine!
Never minding to be patrolled by you, making you the best guard ever! Mother, Oh how I miss conversing with you of life's expectations and struggles. You always shared the best stories, until my stomach hurt. Hitting the nail to point, your voice of experience, I enjoyed listening to. Sent me conquering the world, even if fear filled your heart. Not forgetting your millionaire dress-ups starting with pony tails and sneaks. You always knew when my looks were puzzled and inquisitive.
With the right queue, you picked it up, and with great relief, I shared my heart's distresses. My way of acquiring knowledge, indicating you did an awesome job. You perfected your confidence, and sense of wisdom. Prepared me to face and conquer the world. After your departure, I still can't phantom the idea that you are gone. I waited for your return, like when you used to come home from work. Difference now is that there is no return. Wished it was a bad dream.
In your latter days, there was no way I could not reciprocate all things you taught and showed me. Kept your hopes high even when health was compromised. You are always in my heart; I am an extension of you. Your features intertwine within mine.
Whenever I want to see you, I look in the mirror.
As I smile, I see the smile that once greeted me, for years
Dearest mother you will always live-on for me, you are in my heart and mind. I rejoice today knowing that you gave me the richest life any child could have received. Rest in peace most dearest mom, for you came to earth to project and give love.
Dearest mom, rest assured you excelled, with the greatest task God bestowed upon you.

In Loving Memory of Teofila Castillo

My ♥ Dearest Mom
Mirta Alicia Castillo

Father

I'm in no rush to be a father.

I want to live now and progress much farther.

I want to provide love and discipline.

Not to live without means.

Be an example that he/she can accomplish anything.

I want to be the man that protects them.

Not create a child and neglect them.

I refuse to be associated with resentment.

I want to be there proudly and express how much their date of birth meant.

Teach them the values I were taught.

Help them understand that being there with unconditional love can never be bought.

Have them say my dad is a great man.

Rather than say he's a coward that ran.

I know I won't ever reach perfection.

But I do know I will provide protection, affection, and a sense of direction.

FATHER

Jose Valentin

Lessons Learned

I remember begging you for a quarter.

I realized how fortunate I was when I saw folks in Hondu without running water.

I remember begging for the latest shoes.

I stopped once I saw kids wearing sandals in and out of school.

I remembered begging you for an extra piece of chicken.

I stopped begging when I realized some folks only source of protein was through fishing.

As an adult, I hear kids whining about things they wish they had.

It just reminds me of my past.

Their mindset will change once they realize what's in their grasp.

I gradually stopped being ungrateful
.
I can't take back the times I said, "I hate you".

I am very thankful.

In a few years, I will demonstrate how proud I will make you (Mom).

Lover or Friend

Beautiful, I am and I definitely know; also been told

One, two, three, maybe four reiterate, ooh so beautiful!

Wagging boompsy, will that categorize me sexiest?

Self-assured, never influenced, lady to fullest extent

Choosing you to be friend vs. lover become a breeze

Many lovers? Hmmmm fun, a definite no go, not my mojo

Beautiful sexy lady titled, special to one, two, many

Attached lower your category, to immediate friendship

Her shadow blocks the brightness from my ray of light

True lover picked, which angle will be your approach?

Which body part will he love, eyes, lips, thigh or all?

Entirely is aim, loving wholesomely as a package

One size fits all, no holds barred, with Midas touch

Lover is who love me, spirit, mind, soul and then some

Maximize essence, trust, communication, and honesty

Making me Queen as he rules in God's sacred temple

My King takes all with all due rewards and merit!

LOVER OR FRIEND

Mirta Alicia Castillo

My Dearest Friend

My dearest friend you became

Accepted you, as you did me with all our faults

Even when we see our world upside down

Having love in common, you gained a friend in me, forever.

Your struggles becomes my struggles

A sad day for me becomes same for you

Regardless of what you go through, you have a friend

When you can't climb, I am there to push you to the top

It hurts to hear you or see you cry, I am there with a shoulder

Never had I doubted that I would not receive the same love back

So I safeguard the best gift I've ever been blessed with

Having you as My Dearest Friend!

Dedicated to my dear friend, Rose Avellanet

My Dearest Friend
MIRTA ALICIA CASTILLO

BROKEN BONDS

You were my pudgy sweet little baby
Bundle of joy that brought smile to my face
Sweetening my heart with every treasured day
Looking forward to see you at the end of a work day
Strongest love ever held, touched, to share all with you
You lit up my life as I watched you grow
Now you distance yourself because something I said with good intentions and something you felt hurt you
So why is it hard for you to let go? So I messed up
No one said a parent should be perfect, nor given instructions on how to take care of emotional hurt
I can't see your pain unless you voice it,
Learn to share these emotions or they will destroy you
Being the oldest I had to learn to perfect my parenting skills so not to mess up your other siblings.
You don't want to talk because you choose not to talk
If you felt you wanted to correct things you could have
But your ego is too proud
Blinding you from seeing the love I have for you and potential to build
Why do you rather see me hurting?
I get the impression that you delight in watching me hurt.
What have I said or failed to say to have pulled us apart?
My soul cries to fix, but I'm afraid it is reaching the end
Sweet daughter of mine, I am hoping that your children don't return the favor, because my heart aches
from your distance, wish you understood that you owe me now, especially having given you my all as you
were a child
What do you struggle with? Why do you hold this grudge? Remove the venom that poisons your soul
against mine. How then do I say I love you as I constantly watch your back walking away from me
Would you even care if I share with you that I shed tears from your indifference?
Would you care that I am ailing in my dying bed hoping that God would give us more time to make it
right?
Don't cry later when I'm gone, because you were given the chance to make it right and failed
I know you are strong emotionally because you hold your emotional gun steady and won't let it go. There
is nothing left to do but wish you the best, with your children who are quickly approaching in your rear-
ing and the emotional wall that you've created. Although this hurts, I must learn to let go, goodbye to the
daughter I once had.

Mirta Alicia Castillo

Happy Mother's Day

Mother is one who bears it all
One who always stand tall

Mother comprehends when no one else does
She will withstand even when you are left with foes

Mother has an open door policy
It's the children who close it shut with fallacy

Because of her fruitfulness her strength is immeasurable
Cares for self and as many who treasure

Beautiful inside and out, radiance secure
Treasured, she can win any situation over, for sure

Blessed in every way even when finances are scarce
Faith and belief make her abundantly fierce

Allowing God to intervene in battles, she reverts to being militant
Problem surfaced, its problem solved with persistence

Great love received, and is reciprocated
No hug feel as good nor warm, and most vindicated

There is something about a mother's blessing
As it is given, and received, one can run without staggering

Walking in the same straight line, blessings flourish
Defying her you'll wonder why you feel poverished

Loving and treasuring will grant you great love and support
As a mother pours love into everything, glorify her by returning the same love back, she is deserving of it
every day!

Mirta Alicia Castillo

Lost Brother

Separated at birth, because we were considered savages by the church.

We stood in line while others figure our worth.

We were sent off in different directions.

We received the same treatment for sharing the same complexion.

Years pass by.

We later reunite to realize our cultures have gone by.

We look the same but carry different names.

Mine is English while yours is from Spain.

We both go through daily struggles and endure the same pain.

We look at each other differently.

We can tell we are brothers quite vividly.

Why we can't agree on things remain a mystery.

The conflict dates back from history

Jose Valentin

Missing You Mom

Spoiled me rotten with your motherly love, wish you were still here

Seeing you, thanking you, sharing everything you freely poured into my life

Mom, you made life easier to understand, sequentially enough to patiently wait

As a child you guided, teaching me right from wrong

You knew when I did wrong, for it felt like betrayal, of the most beautiful being I'd ever known

Today I miss you, everyone seem to have an agenda, few even stop to say hello

Grateful to the Almighty to have taken you home to be with Him, for He deemed me ready to face it all

Thank God you prepared me to face the future, because I enjoy mimicking your rich ways

Thank God he made you Garifuna for now I understand my most treasured guardian angel watches over me

My most treasured moments would always have been with you

Forever love you mom even when you are gone to rest.

Mirta Alicia Castillo

MOTHER

I know you are gone
You are as near as before
Tough times, tear drops, doubled by absence
Sweet memory of our love, laughter, long talks
Hearing your voice in my ear, "Todo estará bien hija."
Resonating, loving, accompanied by tight hug
Strong in my weakest moments, you were
God thought I was ready, when He took you
Just for this moment, I lean on memory
Memory that once kept, held, and hugged me
As trouble surface I know where to lean, your love
Ironic, when things go wrong, your memory pacifies
The world don't understand this love for you, mom
Would give anything to have you back
To hear you sing, see your concern, and smile again
Loved being pushed away, for wrecking your nerves
"Beybasayagien Negrita" was your favorite words
I knew that you just wanted me nearer
Exhausted from laughter, I knew when to stop
Can make use of that good ole laughter now
As these tears drop, I'm renewed with happiness
Knowing you once shared this life with me
I smile because you never left, for I am that extension
The beauty you had, I now see in me
Tranquil demeanor, caring for loved ones, I too harbor
Remembering, keeping you present is my reflection
Loving myself as you taught me
Stand proud in God's presence Chiqui!
There is no better place, where a mom like you belong

Mirta Alicia Castillo

TOUGH TIMES

Almost Paradise

I was elated to find out you were close enough to be mine

Ideations of great times ahead became heaven in my mind

Soon interference pulled you away, now you are no longer mine

Because of hatred some people couldn't see me happy, so they pulled you away

Though it hurt my soul, hoping they can give you the love I envisioned for you

God had a purpose introducing me into your life, regret losing you, but don't regret a lesson learned

God made sure of my purpose in your world, it was for you to come and enjoy all he had created on earth

God interfered, this battle was never mine, it was always His

I love you honey, even if I never got to hold you in my arms

It was very close, we almost did make it!

Close enough to a paradise set up for you and me!

Almost Paradise

MIRTA ALICIA CASTILLO

You Can't Handle This

I count on God to keep me intact
I don't know how I make it thru at times, in fact

God grants me knowledge to help me figure out the way
Blesses me so that I have options as I thread along, hurray!

Loving me dearly, so that I mimic Him, so I do the same
Guiding me through the roughest seasons successfully, I proclaim

On the other hand, you can't seem to figure it out, golden
The world taught you, to handle it all on your lonesome

Not to count on no one, but yourself, how lonely
Even those you consider close friends walk-on by, only

In the meantime you are boss and dictate how I should "behave"
I behave in the mannerism God ordains, for my path He paves

Choose not to consider Him in your life; it'll be your loss
You cannot be in two different worlds; you can't handle this "Abuti" (Chief)

You Can't Handle This!

MIRTA ALICIA CASTILLO

Bullied

Constantly told I'm too dark or too ugly.

Taking my self-esteem from me.

Hurtful words to a tormented reality.

Confused in sexuality.

Anytime I eat, people mock and stare and say, "Look what a tragedy"

Get beat up by everyone even esteemed faculty.

Many look from the outside and call me weak.

Dismissing how words can cut so deep.

Leaving many with only one option for peaceful sleep.

Hated for being different.

Judge by the music they listen.

Constantly being judged.

What happened to kindness and love?

Loved and understood by the one above.

Sincerely Voices of the bullied

Jose Valentin

It's Easier to Blame It on the Economy

Economy this and economy that
Blame it all on system malfunction
Brains hired to set-up system malfunction

Economy this and economy that
Uncle Sam hands stretched out
Who controls the grabbing of that?

Economy this and economy that
Big table with no food
Supermarket shelves never remained so full
Refrigerator never held bare minimum
Who lowers prices so that poor can indulge?

Economy this and economy that
Cars barely move, gas so high
Buses and trains never seemed so packed
Did somebody say energy conservation?

Economy this and economy that
Youth determined to be uneducated
Jobs seem more stressful and difficult
Work deem people unworthy
Who lowers tuition to the ones wishing education?

Economy this and economy that
America's health never seemed poor
Health insurance expensively controlled
Who grabs hold of the cost of one's health?

Economy this and economy that
We are the United States of America
With 51 states and not one has a solution
There are boroughs, counties, and cities
Congressmen, Senators, Mayor's hired to do a job
Its easier to blame the President and the economy
How cowardly have we become?

Mirta Alicia Castillo

Movement

Determined to win. Born to lose.

Living life mentally and physically abused.

Look at the environment my parents were forced to choose.

Drug and violence all over the news.

Society does its part to shorten one's views.

Shattered glass of dreams that never came true.

Educators steer some away of what they want to do.

Some use sports as their only outlet.

Not realizing this is the simplest way to become a financial puppet.

Dreams inflated by low self-esteem.

In turn, creates a cycle on unwed parenting teens.

Afraid to ask for help because of the card one is dealt.

Love of life turn into hate.

Substance is used to push life beyond at an uncontrollable rate.

I can only move forward and inspire others in order for my community to be rewarded

Jose Valentin

Physical Abuse

You claim loving me to the core of your heart,
Running away is my only desire, being far, far apart,

Your "love" lifting hands over my body, incongruent,
Screams, tears, and disbelief say you shouldn't?

Aren't I the most treasurable flower to safeguard?
How did I turn to be that thorn, most scarred?

Wishing to scream for the world to learn of my anguish,
Afraid for loved ones, don't want them feeling rubbish,
I keep feeling worse, numbing feeling of garbage,

Keep telling myself maybe one day it'll end,
Hoping his family can see it and maybe defend,

Wish for x-ray vision, mind-reading to scan the experience,
Someone to stop, ask, not necessarily the biggest audience,

Exhausted, trembling from gestures, lunges, anxiety until next episode
Drop, slap, punch taking my breath away, oh Lord what a load!

No, not my son or daughter dropping to the ground as I bawl,
Resisting, looking to the sky in great pain,
Hoping for the next, and not the last, tear drop to fall!

Mirta Alicia Castillo

Untold

I don't know if I should be upset or understanding.

I felt as if my elders left me hanging.

Pretending it wasn't there.

Maybe they didn't care.

Maybe it was designed for me not to be aware.

Maybe it was subtly said when I was told life wasn't fair.

I wish I was more prepared.

I overcame painful lessons.

Leaving me with so many questions.

I guess it was ignored because they were soon going home.

Leaving me to learn this reality on my own.

It would have helped to be informed.

I would have been prepared to fight.

Rather than initially accept it as being the norm.

Jose Valentin

UNCERTAINTY

Choices

I walked here and there.

Absorbed many cold stares.

Considered America's worst nightmare.

A man of color with a mind.

Some say I'm wise beyond my time.

Fortunate not to be raised around the "no child left behind"

Others only have money on their mind.

The trap of elite leaves them blind.

Focusing on material possessions.

While the few continue running every election.

Tangible things can be taken away from me.

My mind is what kept me away from slavery.

Is what makes me different.

Raised by Garifunas who taught me to listen.

Powerful attributes, discipline and wisdom.

Lessons that kept me from prison.

Defiant Choices

Life valued less than a pair of sneakers.

More becoming followers than actual leaders.

Opting not to read.

Afraid to lead.

Believing in failure of the implanted seed.

Knowledge is an important tool.

It's taught in and out of school.

Many lessons of how the world can be so cruel.

Ignorance is strengthening.

Sentences are lengthening.

Some are losing hope.

Some are using violence to cope.

Some are at the end of their rope.

Happiness is rare.

No one cares.

Hopefully I wake up from this nightmare.

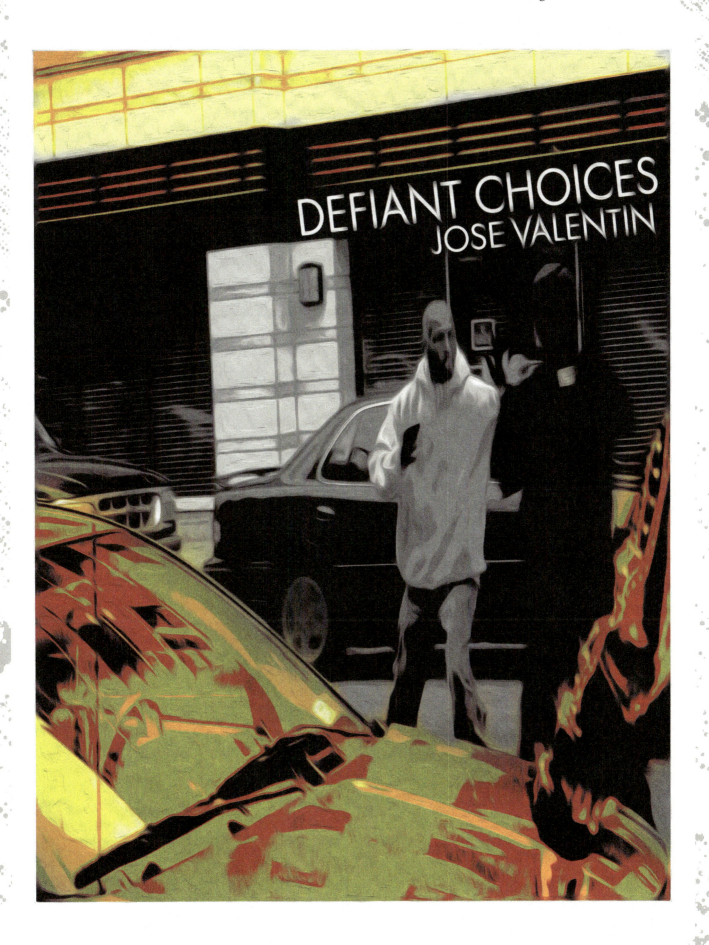

DIVISIVE THOUGHTS

Mind is blank and stuck
Unsure of what has struck

Confused of which road to take
Any wrong move made, will put me at stake

Familiar road it seems, have to try not to repeat
Because this will definitely lead to another defeat

Both roads promising in the beginning
Whose to know what lie ahead, how deceiving

My mind, heart, and soul is set on doing right
Oh Lord, help me, I plea you make it bright

For I have always known you never leave me
Nor have ever forsaken me

All I have to do is take the road, for you will lead
Even if I thought it was the wrong one I heed

Mind clarity it's what you have always been about,
There is no confusion about you Father, none!

MIRTA ALICIA CASTILLO

DIVISIVE THOUGHTS

Finding Oneself

I remember the first day I was searched.

I knew being black that I was born as a curse.

Believing in it made it worse.

Idolizing the dudes on the block.

I joined forces and hated the enemy, the cops.

I grew up believing I was something that I wasn't.

I went to hondu one summer.

It began to make me wonder.

I was headed towards a path of becoming a number.

I saw people with a limited water and light.

From that moment on, I began to do right.

Gradually gave up smoking and drinking.

So that common sense could finally sink in.

I saw my peers go through the same.

Unlike them, I wasn't deported.

I began living life with a purpose.

Throwing my life away through my parents sacrifice wasn't worth it.

I stopped making excuses.

They all became useless.

Perseverance in heart and mind is where truth lives.

Finding Oneself

JOSE VALENTIN

Overcoming!!!

God, Thank You For My Gift

Most beautiful ray of sunshine newly introduced into life,

Barely visible; dim from wretchedness of storm's strife,

Fog extremely thick to envision at any distance,

It is true God is one, only, who paves path with consistence,

Waited for thunderstorm seizing, and torrential outpouring rain,

Gray skies dissipated as our special day for meeting came,

With great disbelief, from becoming a possibility of what I've always wanted,

Through it all I never got it, disappointed,

Doubting everyone who came with miraculous news,

No way did I flinch, nor cause me to believe or choose,

"Do you want to be mommy for my granddaughter?"

Uttered words sounding foreign, as tears flowed, mind occupied in disbelief,

How could it be? I've been battered by the greatest grief?

Place where rain couldn't drop any more, or plea any longer,

God! You never forgot my plea, tears, and here suddenly making me believe,

So impactful as God set you in my path, you are tender, tiny and yet lovely.

Just as I had once imagined many years ago!

You are the most beautiful and valued gift I ever unwrapped in my lifetime!

It was worthwhile weathering the storm to be blessed with you!

God our Father, Thank You for my daughter!

God, Thank You For My Gift!

God, Thank You For My Gift

Mirta Alicia Castillo

The Legacy Continues

It was never about me,
For you shared your love with all those respecting your views,

Burying my pain became agenda of utmost importance, to let go of the blues,

Missing the two beings who enjoyed seeing me at my best,

Smile and love radiating now, reflecting beautiful memories, while remaining blessed,

Pain clouded thoughts, imagery of "misfortune", for all along, God made sure all was addressed,

Their exit from this world, I wasn't forgotten and will always be memorable,

Living the greatest reflection of their love and teaching, for they were impressionable,

Because God calls all shots of life, their time was now here,

Bringing them to heaven four months apart, seeming unreal!

Now as clear as day, and bright as my mind, I let go,

Leaving behind love, security, assurance, strength, stability though,

It wasn't easy, but thankful to God Almighty for pulling me through life's greatest pain,

Remembering good times and educational ones, eased the feeling of drain,

Living their legacy is everything I envision,

Loving, being proud, and approval of me was all their provision,

They gave it to the greatest degree!

Opening up to new beginnings, to God I plea,

Placing lessons into practice, until we meet again, the legacy continues!

Loved them with all my might, they were my tightest crew!

Thank you, Teofila and Silvio Castillo, for all the love I was born and reared into, I love you both, rest in peace, for God know you did the most outstanding job you ever could!

Your legacy continues!

Mirta Alicia Castillo

About the Authors

Mirta Alicia Castillo, was born in Honduras, and migrated at age eight to Bronx, New York. She was educated and reared in the New York educational system. She graduated as a Registered Nurse with a Baccalaureate degree in Nursing from the City College of New York. Working as a nurse, she realized nursing was not all that was cut out for her; there was a part of her that was missing from just being in the healthcare field. It was not until hardship struck; finding herself caught up in the webs of her own marital problems and both parents suffering from progressively debilitating chronic diseases. As the years progressed, and unfortunately as being the process of life, both parents passed away four months apart; leading her into eminent and an inevitable separation from her husband as well. At this time, she realized that writing relieved her stressors, anxieties and sorrows. Without getting the opportunity to mourn accordingly; her new acquired strength was channeled into writing for Garifuna culture, everything she had already grown to know, and learned about poetry, different topics affecting the Garifuna community, male and female relational issues, focusing primarily on relationships , many motivational and inspirational topics on Facebook's, GarifunaTV Page. The trials in her life, such as marital problems, death of both parents, pain caused by those claiming to love her, forced and strengthened her to find a different modality of coping and managing her emotions. The poems within *Drumming The Beat To Our Emotions* are reflective of this time period in her life, Garifuna culture, and the starting- over phase, after the storms in her life.

Her faith in God kept her head above water, knowing for certainty that she was never going to get entirely consumed by the storms in her life. She is hoping that *Drumming The Beat To Our Emotions* will also help you deal with the storms of your life. She is elated to have overcome this phase in her life and is looking forward to bringing forth Mirta Alicia Castillo to a brighter, happier, and more victorious limelight!

Co-Author:

Jose Valentin was born and raised in Harlem, New York, in a Honduran household, held together by a single mother. Growing up in the inner city, he had to overcome much adversity. He learned about the endless opportunities he had in comparison to individuals living in Honduras. After visiting Limon Honduras, he further comprehended the opportunities he possessed as a naturalized citizen of the United States.

In the inner city, one is taught to accept the arbitrariness that occurs within the community. In reality, change is not made unless people challenge the unjust practices of society. The clear unjust actions made by police officers against inner city youth propelled him to write about the experiences endured by young men. Also the effect the media has on today's society.

He admires people like Thurgood Marshall, John F. Kennedy, and Martin Luther king Jr, who viewed law as a means to change the social structure of society. Understanding who he is a Garifuna man and also motivated him to write. The creation of Garifunatv Page opened a forum for Jose to express his thoughts.

CPSIA information can be obtained
at www.ICGtesting.com
Printed in the USA
LVOW02s2100200916

505475LV00001B/1/P

9 781496 924476